A GRAND NEW DAY

A GRAND NEW DAY

IT'S NEVER TOO LATE TO BEGIN AGAIN

Margaret Feinberg

Foreword by Sheila Walsh

THOMAS NELSON
Since 1798

NASHVILLE   DALLAS   MEXICO CITY   RIO DE JANEIRO   BEIJING

Published in Nashville, Tennessee, by Thomas Nelson. Thomas Nelson is a trademark of Thomas Nelson, Inc.

Thomas Nelson, Inc., titles may be purchased in bulk for educational, business, fund-raising, or sales promotional use. For information, please e-mail SpecialMarkets@ThomasNelson.com.

ISBN: 978-1-4185-3412-7

Printed in China

09 10 11 12 MT 5 4 3 2 1

Contents

Contents

Foreword

There is something about the word *new* that has always been appealing to me. Whether it was the opportunity to start a new diet or try a new face cream or read a book by a new author, the word itself seems full of hope. This hope can quickly turn to disappointment however when the promise offered falls far short of our expectations. I received a free sample in the mail of a cream that was supposed to turn back the clock and make me look fifteen years younger, but after using it for the suggested two-week period I could see absolutely no difference whatsoever. Perhaps I needed a new mirror or new eyes! This world makes many promises and delivers very few. I'm sure you could add to my list with your own experiences that have been disappointing.

That will never be true though with God our Father. One of the reasons that I am very excited that you decided to pick up this study is that whatever your hopes and expectations are of what God might have in store for you, you will not be disappointed. Scripture tells us that, "Eye has not seen, nor ear heard, nor have entered into the heart of man the things which God has prepared for those who love Him" (1 Corinthians 2:9 NKJV).

But what if your disappointment is with yourself? You may have a track record of trying over and over to change behavior patterns or remain true to new ones, but what greets you in the mirror is not disappointment with a new product but with yourself. I wonder if there is anything more prevalent among Christian women than guilt? We expect so much of ourselves. We want to be the best daughters or moms or friends that we can be and set standards that are hard to maintain. When you add in the desire to live a life that would always be pleasing and honoring to God, that is quite a load to carry. Jesus was very tuned in to our tendency to over-burden ourselves and it was his passionate mission to teach us how to live a new way.

"Are you tired? Worn out? Burned out on religion? Come to me. Get away with me and you'll recover your life. I'll show you how to take a real rest. Walk with me and work with me—watch how I do it. Learn the unforced rhythms of grace. I won't lay anything heavy or ill-fitting on you. Keep company with me and you'll learn to live freely and lightly."
—Matthew 11:28–30

I love the invitation to learn how to live freely and lightly! That truly is a magnificent promise. As you move through this study may God give you new hope, clear vision and a trusting heart. He doesn't expect us to get it all right, but rather live in the truth that he has finished the work for us and thrown open the doors to a grand new day.

—Sheila Walsh

Introduction

The Best is Yet to Come!

There's a story told of a young a man who grew up in a loving home. On occasion, his family would go out for a meal at a restaurant. As the family finished enjoying their meals, the young man's father would lean over and gently remind him, "Don't order the apple pie!"

Now the father never said this to discourage his son from ordering dessert, but rather to protect him from disappointment. The father had learned over the years that not even the finest of restaurants could ever compete with his wife's apple pie. The father wanted his son to know that the best apple pie always came from the same source—his mother's kitchen.

In the same way, the best possible things in life always come from the same source: God. He is the ultimate source of our hope, peace, and joy. He promises us not just life, but abundant life. And there are no substitutions that can compete or compare. Like the father in the story, our Heavenly Father gently reminds us, "Don't settle for less than My best!"

What does that mean in our daily lives? It means that what's happened in the past is not what defines us. No matter what we've done or left undone—no matter what mistakes, errors, or blunders—nothing is beyond God's redemption!

No matter where we are in our spiritual journeys, God invites us to something more. No matter what age or stage of life you're in—single or married, working or retired, raising children or left with an empty nest—God has a grand new day planned for you. He has something original and one-of-a-kind picked out just for you! He wants to use you and the special gifts He has given you to encourage others, to make the world a better place, and to help others encounter God.

And the best part is that you don't have to wait until tomorrow to begin experiencing the grand new day God has for you. It can begin today. As you connect with God through prayer and this study, you just might be surprised to discover that the plans He has for you begin right now, on this very day. Best of all, there's no telling what adventure God may set you on—in your relationships, your home, and your faith journey.

My hope and prayer is that through this study you'll discover the grand new day God has for you—one filled with redemption, restoration, and hope. And that you'll find yourself refusing to settle for any substitutions, waiting on God for all He wants to do in and through you for years to come!

Blessings,

Margaret Feinberg

All Things New

This first section will look at the fresh start that
is available to us every day. One of the delights of
being a follower of God is that we have the privilege
of rediscovering God's goodness, including His
grace and mercy, every single day. That kind of
realization can help us shift our understanding, our
perspective, and even the way we live our lives.

One

The Wake–Up Call

Because of the Lord's great love we are not
consumed, for his compassions never fail. They are
new every morning; great is your faithfulness.

LAMENTATIONS 3:22–23

The phone rings early in the morning. You reach over and pick up the receiver. A familiar voice simply says three words: "Were you sleeping?"

Though it's a simple, straight-forward question, all of us have probably struggled to answer from time to time. We may tell the person asking that we were "just resting our eyes" or "nodding off." But we still know that we weren't wide awake when the person called.

Just as a friend can wake us up with an early morning phone call to let us know something important, God invites us to wake up to the reality of Him every day. It's true. Whether you recognize it or not, you received a call from God this morning. The Bible says that

God's mercies are new every morning. And that's a piece of news you can't afford to miss.

God invites us to wake up to the reality of His presence in our lives each and every day. He may get our attention through all kinds of unexpected ways. He may speak through a passage of the Bible you're reading. He may answer a prayer you've been waiting on for weeks, months, or years. He may share a much-needed word of encouragement with you through a friend. God is incredibly creative when it comes to awakening our hearts to His love.

> *God is incredibly creative when it comes to awakening our hearts to His love.*

So the question is: Did you receive the wake-up call today? Or did you roll over in bed? Were you tempted to push snooze? Or have you had your heart awakened to the amazing love God has for you and the reality that He wants to do so much more in your life than you can possibly dream or imagine?

God is issuing you a wake-up call—even if you're not a morning person. He is worth getting out of bed for and getting to know. He has a grand new day planned for you and it begins today.

1. Do you tend to be a morning person or a night owl? Explain.

2. *Are there any areas of your life in which you feel God has been trying to awaken your heart?*

3. *Are there any areas of your life in which you feel God has been trying to awaken your heart but you have been trying to roll over and go back to bed?*

Throughout the Gospels, we read incredible stories of Jesus offering a grand new day to those He encountered. He often performed miracles, and in the process of healing and restoring lives, Jesus offered a wake-up call not only to the people who were healed but also the surrounding communities. This was particularly true when Jesus encountered a paralytic.

4. Read **Mark 2:1–12**. What was the wake-up call that the paralytic received from Jesus in this passage (verse 5 and 11)? How did the paralytic respond? How do you think his life was changed?

5. Other than the paralytic in this passage, who else received a wake-up call that God was doing something new? (See verses 3, 6–7, and 12.)

The greatest wake-up call in the New Testament, the grandest of all grand new days, is the moment when Jesus arose from the dead. When the news of Jesus' resurrection spread, it sent shockwaves throughout the surrounding community and eventually around the world.

6. Read *Matthew 28:1–20*. How does the Bible describe Mary
   Magdalene and the other Mary's response to the angel's news
   of the empty tomb (verse 8)? How does the Bible describe their
   response to Jesus' appearance (verses 9–10)? Now take a few
   moments to imagine how you would have responded. Describe
   those feelings in the space below.

7. After rising from the dead, Jesus gives His disciples a very clear
   commission in verses 19–20. Write that commission in the
   space below:

8. *Have you ever had a time when God awakened you to the reality of Him and then called you to do something specific as a response? If so, explain.*

> *God's mercies are new every morning! He awakens us to the reality of His presence in our lives and invites us to know Him even more.*

Digging Deeper

It's amazing to think of all that God has done in people's lives. Read *Mark 10:46–52*. Spend some time reflecting on the story of a blind man, Bartimaeus, and his encounter with Jesus. Does anything strike you as particularly compelling from this story? Why do you think it's so important to tell God what we want or need from Him? Why do you think Bartimaeus's response was to follow Jesus?

Ponder and Pray

The opening scripture for this lesson comes from Lamentations 3:22–23: "Because of the Lord's great love we are not consumed, for his compassions never fail. They are new every morning; great is your faithfulness." In what ways have you found this passage to be true in your own life? Why do you think it's important to pursue a relationship with God every morning?

Bonus Activity

Spend some time reflecting on any wake-up calls that you feel God has been giving you over the past few months. Are there things you need to change in your life? Any habits? Things you want to stop doing or feel like you need to do more? Make a list of one to three things you'd like to do to usher in a grand new day. Now prayerfully consider what changes you'll need to make to make those a reality.

Two

Awakened

Therefore, if anyone is in Christ, he is a new creation; the old has gone, the new has come!

2 CORINTHIANS 5:17

Have you ever listened to a great motivational speaker? They probably made you feel inspired, ready to take greater risks or work even harder. But studies show that all too often these effects are short lived. People may get excited in the moment, but all too often the energy fizzles out if it isn't focused in a particular direction or initiative.

So now that you've received the wake-up call, the invitation to a grand new day, how do you respond? What do you do next? How do you move from just having your heart awakened to actually helping awaken in the hearts of others?

The truth is there is no one-size-fits-all answer! Everyone responds to God's presence in their lives differently. For some, embracing a new beginning may mean reconnecting with family or friends where those relationships have long since faded. For others, it may mean getting plugged into a faith community for the first time ever or the first time in many years. For still others, it may be found in a change of heart about a situation or person. But the key to embracing that new beginning and starting fresh is making a change! Whether that change manifests itself in your attitude or your actions, it's one of the signs that you're moving forward and embracing all that God has for you.

The key to embracing that new beginning and starting fresh is making a change!

That's the beauty of a grand new day—it's available to every person in unique and fresh ways. We all have one awaiting us. That may mean choosing to do something new or try something different. It may mean making time for something we chose to hurry by before. All of us will embrace our grand new days in different ways, and they're all worth celebrating.

1. *How do you respond to change? Do you tend to enjoy it or try to avoid it?*

2. *Think about a time when you made a major change in your life and embraced a new opportunity. What were the circumstances surrounding that change? What compelled you to make a change?*

Throughout the Gospels, we read of many women and men who Jesus encountered and offered them a grand new day. He gave them the opportunity to start fresh and live their lives in a whole new way. One of those was the woman who was caught in adultery.

3. *Read John 8:1–11. What is the most powerful aspect of this story to you?*

4. *After the crowd left and Jesus was left standing alone with the woman, He told her to do something specific. What were His instructions (verse 11)? Why do you think this instruction is so important when it comes to embracing what God has for you?*

5. *Do you think it's possible to embrace the grand new day God has for you if you willingly choose to continue sinning? Why or why not?*

6. Read **John 4:1–42**. How would you describe the woman in the well? On the lines below, make a list of adjectives describing the woman at the well.

_____   _____

_____   _____

_____   _____

_____   _____

7. What was the woman's response to her initial interaction with Jesus (verses 28–30)? What was the Samaritans' response to the woman's story (verses 39–41)?

The woman at the well experienced a grand new day because of her encounter with Jesus, but she didn't keep the news to herself. She returned to her hometown to tell her friends and family. As a result, many of them encountered a grand new day themselves.

8. Why do you think it's important to share the stories of your encounters with God and the grand new days He gives you with others? Have you ever had an experience like the Samaritan woman where you shared your faith and others came to know Jesus as a result? If so, describe them below.

> God's wants to give each of us a fresh start, but in order to embrace all that He has for us, we have to respond. Often that response includes making a change—whether it's in our habits, our choices, or our attitudes. Sometimes that means we must stop doing things that go against God's commands or start doing things God asks. But the rewards are worth it all!

Digging Deeper

God wants to do amazing things in and through all of our lives. Read Mark 2:22. Why do you think it's important to be ready and willing to respond to God's nudges in our lives? Why is it important to be willing to make a change in our personal and spiritual lives? What changes do you feel God is calling you to make in your own life?

Ponder and Pray

The opening scripture for this lesson comes from 2 Corinthians 5:17: "Therefore, if anyone is in Christ, he is a new creation; the old has gone, the new has come!" How have you found this passage to be true in your own life? Are there any ways in which you feel like you are holding onto your old life? Is there anything stopping you from embracing the new?

Bonus Activity

Spend some time reflecting on how your relationship with God has really changed you. On a piece of paper, place the word "New" on one side of the page and "Old" on the other side of the page. Draw a line down the middle. Now make a list of how the "new" you in Christ is different from the "old" you. Even if you've been a follower of Jesus your entire life, there are still ways in which God is growing you, changing you, and making you new in Him. Record them. Then spend some time thanking God for the work He is doing in you.

Three

Fresh Perspective

*Immediately, something like scales fell from Saul's
eyes, and he could see again.*

ACTS 9:18

Author and teacher Tony Campolo tells a compelling story of a
bum he met in Philadelphia. The man had not bathed and was covered in soot, but his most distinguishing characteristic was his long
beard that was matted with food. While walking by, Campolo heard
the man offer him some of his coffee.

Slightly caught off guard, Campolo accepted the offer as a kind
gesture, but guessed the man probably had ulterior motives. He asked
what compelled the man to share. The homeless man explained that
the coffee seemed particularly good that morning and he figured that
if God gives you something good that you should share it with others. Figuring the man was going to solicit him for money, Campolo
asked him if there was anything he could give him.

Unexpectedly, the man asked for a hug.

The homeless man proceeded to bear hug Campolo. It felt like the man was never going to let go. People began to stare. But suddenly, the awareness of others transformed into an awareness of God and the words of Jesus, "For I was hungry and you gave me something to eat, I was thirsty and you gave me something to drink, I was a stranger and you invited me in, I needed clothes and you clothed me, I was sick and you looked after me, I was in prison and you came to visit me" (Matthew 25:35–36).

Sometimes the grand new day God gives us isn't visibly spectacular on the outside, yet there is something significant that shifts inside us.

For Tony Campolo, loving God on that day in Philadelphia meant giving a bum a hug. The experience forever changed his perspective on what it means to truly love. While not as dramatic, all of us have God-designed experiences that change the way we understand and interact with the world around us.

Sometimes the grand new day God gives us isn't visibly spectacular on the outside, yet there is something significant that shifts inside us. We find ourselves thinking differently, responding differently, and living differently. We find that the grand new day has not overwhelmed as much as snuck up on us, but it still changes us forever. Indeed, some of the most amazing things that happen to us can't be seen on the outside, but only on the inside as we shift our perspective to align more with God's own.

1. Have you ever had an experience like the one described with the homeless man—one that changed the way you see others?

2. *Have you ever worked with the poor or those in need? What lessons did you learn from them about life? Faith? God?*

3. *When was the last time your perspective changed on an issue or situation? Did the change result in more or less compassion for others? Explain.*

4. *Read **Ezekiel 11:19**. Do you think your heart is currently more stone or more flesh? Explain.*

5. Why do you think it's so important to have a "heart of flesh"? In what ways did Jesus demonstrate what it looked like to have a "heart of flesh"?

On the road to Emmaus, two people had an unexpected encounter with Jesus that changed their lives and their perspectives on faith forever.

6. Read **Luke 24:13–34**. Do you think the two people on the road to Emmaus were in a good place to encounter Jesus in their journeys and conversations? Why or why not?

7. *What were the disciples' responses to what Jesus shared to them (verse 32)? Have you ever had the "burning heart" sensation described?*

Though nothing changed specifically on that day on the road to Emmaus, something significant happened in those two men's hearts. They encountered Jesus and they simply could not be the same.

8. *How do you think those two men's lives were different after the encounter with Jesus? How has your own life been different since you encountered Jesus?*

God's wants to give each of us a fresh perspective. He wants us to see things as He sees them and love others as He loves them. When we embrace a change in perspective, things deep down inside of us shift and we're better able to reflect God to the world around us.

Digging Deeper

One of the greatest shifts in perspective that we can have is knowing who we are as children of God. Read *Hebrews 10:20–22*. How does it make you feel to know that God has made a way for you to draw near to Him? Are you actively pursuing a relationship with God or holding back? Have you embraced all the forgiveness, grace, and mercy God has for you? Why or why not?

Ponder and Pray

The opening scripture for this lesson comes from Acts 9:18: "Immediately, something like scales fell from Saul's eyes, and he could see again." The story of Saul who became Paul is a compelling one. Read his conversion story in Acts 9:1–31. If God can transform someone like Saul, do you think there's anyone who is beyond his redemption? Explain. Is there anyone on whom you have given up hope who God is calling you pray for or reach out to?

Bonus Activity

Serving others is an amazing way to shift our perspective toward others and God. If you aren't involved as a volunteer already, look for a way to give to those in need this week. Consider spending time working at a local soup kitchen, donating to charity, or visiting a home for the elderly.

Looking at the Past through the Rearview Mirror

This second session is a reminder that God makes

all things new every day. That means what

happened yesterday is truly yesterday's news. God

wants you to move forward today, tomorrow, and

beyond to become all that you were created to be.

Four

The Beauty of Redemption

Because by one sacrifice he has made perfect forever
those who are being made holy.

Hebrews 10:14

There once was a boy who took his small handcrafted boat to the local river. He placed the boat in the water and smiled widely as the boat sailed smoothly along. He kept a long string on the boat, so he wouldn't lose his precious creation. Holding the string, he felt the warm sunshine on his face, and enjoyed the sight of his boat floating along in the water.

Without warning, a strong current caught the boat. The young boy tried to hold onto the string, but it broke and the tiny boat was carried downstream. Though the boy tried to keep up with his boat by running along the shore, the current was too fast and it disappeared in the water. The young boy searched everywhere, but finally gave up and returned home.

Several days passed. On his way home from school the young boy decided by chance to look in a store window, and was amazed when he saw a boat just like his. As he got closer he recognized the vessel—it was his boat. The young boy told the store manager that he had made the boat that was in the window and it belonged to him.

The manager explained that someone else had brought it in that morning. If the boy wanted it, then he would have to buy it for one dollar just like any other customer. The boy ran home and gathered all his money. He had one dollar exactly. He returned to the store and purchased his boat. Walking out of the store, he said, "You're twice mine. First, I made you and now I bought you."

The story is a wonderful illustration of the idea of redemption. God did not just make us but He purchased us for a price—the death of His own Son, Jesus. Through that one act of extreme sacrifice, we can become His forever and enter into a relationship that lasts for all of eternity. That means that no matter what you've done or what you've left undone, you can be forgiven. You can move into all that God has for you. Redemption is a gift from God you don't want to miss!

> *God did not just make us but He purchased us for a price—the death of His own Son, Jesus.*

1. *What does it mean to you to know that God was willing to pay a very high price—the death of Jesus—in order to have a relationship with you?*

2. *Are there any parts of your life or your past where you struggle to accept God's forgiveness or have a hard time seeing any redemption? Explain.*

King David was known as a man after God's own heart, yet he committed adultery with a woman by the name of Bathsheba. Yet what we discover through his story is that no one is beyond redemption.

3. *Read 2 Samuel 11. Though David didn't kill Uriah with his own hands, how was he still responsible for his death?*

God uses the prophet Nathan to confront David regarding the murder and adultery. Yet Nathan communicates the message in an unusual way.

4. Read *2 Samuel 12:1–12*. Why do you think Nathan used a story to confront David? Do you think this was effective? Why or why not?

5. Read *2 Samuel 12:13–24*. What was David's response to Nathan's confrontation? What does this passage teach us about sin and repentance?

Despite David's error, God allowed David and his wife Bathsheba to have a second son and they named him Solomon. He became a great leader and the wisest man on earth. What could have turned into a tragedy became a compelling story of redemption and restoration. Another beautiful portrait of redemption is found in the story of Peter who denied Jesus three times.

6. Read **Luke 22:31–34**. Why do you think Jesus warns Peter of what is about to happen to him? What do Jesus' words reveal about his love for Peter?

7. Read **Luke 22:54–62**. Which details of this passage are most interesting to you? What do you think was the primary reason that Peter denied Jesus?

Yet even after denying Jesus, Peter is one of the first to respond to the news of His resurrection.

8. Read *Luke 22:9–12*. What compelled Peter to run to the tomb? What does Peter's response reveal about his desire for a relationship with God?

God's redemption is truly beautiful. God can make all things new. No matter what has happened in the past, nothing is beyond His redeeming power.

Digging Deeper

The redemption that is available to us through Jesus Christ is amazing. Read Galatians 3:12–14. In what ways have you experienced the blessings of God? In what ways have you seen your life change since becoming a follower of Jesus? Do you believe that God can make all things new? Why or why not?

Ponder and Pray

The opening scripture for this lesson comes from *Hebrews 10:14*: "Because by one sacrifice he has made perfect forever those who are being made holy." In what ways are you tempted to wrestle with perfectionism? Do you recognize that God has made you perfect through what Christ has done? Why or why not?

Bonus Activity

Everyone has a beautiful story of redemption in their life. In one page or less, write down a moment in your life when you recognize God's redemption at work. Share your story with at least one person this week.

Five

The Fuel of Forgiveness

If you, O Lord, kept a record of sins, O Lord, who
could stand? But with you there is forgiveness;
therefore you are feared.

PSALM 130:3–4

Thirty-nine American seamen lost their lives in the Persian Gulf when an Iraqi pilot shot at their ship in May 1987. One of photos taken and printed in newspapers was of a five-year-old boy standing with his hand on his heart as his father's coffin was loaded onto a plane to return to the United States. The boy's mother was confident that her husband—who had a relationship with Jesus—was in a better place.

In a compelling response to tragedy, the mother and the boy sent a letter and an Arabic New Testament to the pilot of the Iraqi plane along with a note that let the pilot know they did not hold a grudge and were praying for him. The story is a rich portrait of forgiveness.

In all of our lives we encounter moments when it seems hard, if not impossible, to forgive. But with God all things are possible. And looking at just how much each of us has been forgiven can help us open our hearts to forgiving others. There are times all of us find ourselves struggling to say the words "I forgive you"—and really mean them. But there are also times when we are the ones who need to be forgiven. In our less-than-becoming moments, we may say or do things that hurt others. That's one thing that makes forgiveness so unique: it is something we both give and receive. And to move forward into all that God has for us we need to choose to do both.

Forgiveness allows us to let go of the past and embrace the wondrous tomorrow God has planned all along.

Your grand new day is filled with forgiveness. Forgiveness allows us to let go of the past and embrace the wondrous tomorrow God has planned all along. When we forgive, we say goodbye to what was and say hello to all that God intends.

1. When you think about your relationships, what are some of the easiest things for you to forgive? What are some of the hardest?

2. *When you think about forgiveness, do you find it harder to forgive someone else or yourself? Explain.*

3. *In what ways does unforgiveness keep you in the past and prevent you from embracing a grand new day?*

4. *Read **Matthew 18:21–22**. Does anything surprise you about Jesus' answer to Peter's question (verse 22)?*

5. Why do you think Jesus calls us to forgive so many times?

6. Read *Matthew 18:23–35*. Can you think of a time in your life when you've been the master in the story? Can you think of a time in your life when you've been the servant who owed ten thousand talents (what would translate today into millions of dollars)?

7. When have you been the fellow servant who owed one hundred denari (a couple dollars)?

8. *Is there anyone in your life who you need to forgive right now? What is stopping you from forgiving that person?*

> *Forgiveness goes both ways. Not only do we extend forgiveness to others, but we also receive it as a gift. Forgiveness plays an integral role in letting go of the past and moving forward into all God intends.*

Digging Deeper

Forgiveness is possible through Jesus. Read Acts 13:37–39. In what ways has Jesus made forgiveness available to you? In what ways have you accepted God's forgiveness? Are there any ways in which you've refused God's forgiveness in your life?

Ponder and Pray

The opening scripture for this lesson comes from Psalm 130:3–4: "If you, O Lord, kept a record of sins, O Lord, who could stand? But with you there is forgiveness; therefore you are feared." How does it make you feel to know that forgiveness is found in God? How does that make you want to know or love God more?

Bonus Activity

Often we may find ourselves harboring unforgiveness toward someone without even realizing it. Take out a piece of paper and a pen. Then spend some time in prayer asking God if there is anyone who you need to forgive. Does anyone come to mind? If so, write their names on the piece of paper. Then spend some time in prayer asking God if there is anyone from whom you need to ask forgiveness. Write their names on a piece of paper. Prayerfully consider forgiving—as well as asking forgiveness—for those on your list.

Six

Pressing the Gas Pedal

Be strong and take heart,
all you who hope in the Lord.

PSALM 31:24

Born in England in 1832, James was the son of a Methodist minister. The young boy had his rebellious days, but James's mother faithfully prayed that her son would become a Christian. As a teenager, one day James discovered a small pamphlet that told the story of one man's conversion. The story was so compelling that James invited God to come into his heart. While James's mother had been praying for his son's salvation, James's father had been praying for his son to serve in the mission field in China. God faithfully answered that prayer in 1854 when James decided to serve as a missionary and travel to China.

In 1860, James returned to England with his new wife and spent several years translating the New Testament into a specific Chinese dialect. In 1866, James returned to China with sixteen other mission-aries and founded the China Inland Mission. In 1870, his wife and two of their children died of cholera, but James remained in China. Over the course of his life, James Hudson Taylor established dozens of mission stations, brought more than eight hundred missionaries to the area, and became one of the most widely recognized missionaries in the history of China. Prayer was the catalyst that changed one man's life and has inspired young men and women for years to come.

James Hudson Taylor had no idea what grand new day awaited him when he left his home for China—he had no idea that it would lead him to years of service, faithfulness, and hard work. But undoubtedly, there were moments of exhilaration as he prepared for the adventure, packed, traveled, and settled into the new culture. He chose to move forward from all that he had known to embrace all that God had for him.

> *He chose to move forward from all that he had known to embrace all that God had for him.*

Embracing a grand new day sometimes means pressing the gas pedal of life and trying something new, stepping out in faith, or looking for fresh opportunities to serve. Like James Hudson Taylor, there's no telling what adventures await, but in responding to God's call and leading, you never know how He will use you.

1. *When was the last time you felt God nudging you to do something or try something new? How did you respond? What was the result?*

2. *Though James Hudson Taylor traveled across the world to make a difference, there are countless ways you can make a difference in your own community. What are some great ways you know of to get involved and serve in your area?*

God called Abraham to step out in faith and move forward with his life in a brave and exciting way. God gave him specific directions to leave his home, yet never even told him where he was going!

3. *Read **Genesis 12:1–7**. How hard do you think it was for Abraham (Abram) to follow God? Do you think he had any protest from his family? Do you think he ever second-guessed his decision? Why or why not?*

4. *What would your reaction be if you were suddenly told to move to a new city and start a completely new life?*

5. *How would your reaction be different if you knew it was what God wanted for you?*

God also called Peter to step out in faith and do extraordinary things—to even walk on water!

6. *Read John 14:22–36. How do you think you would have responded to seeing Jesus walk on water toward your boat in a storm?*

7. In what areas of your life do you find it most difficult to step out of the boat and trust God? Circle the responses that are most appropriate:

Family	Retirement	Finances	The Future
Relationships	Health	Work	Scheduling
Children	Other _____		

8. In what areas of your life is it easiest to step out of the boat and pursue what God has for you?

> *Moving forward into all that God has for you can be challenging. We have to make sure that we are asking for and listening to wise counsel and lining up our final destination with God's Word. But once we have, we need to press the gas pedal and go for it!*

Digging Deeper

Paul discovered that God could be trusted with everything, including his life. Read Philippians 4:12–13. How have you found these verses to be true in your own life? Do you think you really can do everything through God? Why or why not?

Ponder and Pray

The opening scripture for this lesson comes from Psalm 31:24: "Be strong and take heart, all you who hope in the Lord." On a scale of one to ten, how strong in hope do you feel right now? Why is it important to hope in the Lord? What happens when you hope in things other than the Lord?

Bonus Activity

Prayerfully consider how God may be asking you to press the gas pedal in your life and try something new. Are there any activities, volunteer opportunities, or needs in your community that you can get involved in? Is there someone new in your community who could use a warm welcome from you? Get out there and try something new to help someone else.

Rediscovering the Spark

Often as we move forward into a grand new day,

we'll find God sparking something inside of us.

But what does that look like? What does that

mean? This section will look at the importance of

prayer and hope in entering a grand new day.

Seven

Praying for God's Best

How gracious he will be when you cry for help! As soon as he hears, he will answer you.

ISAIAH 30:19

Living in a small town in Texas, Clara Frasher watched hundreds of students walk to the high school located across the street each morning. Looking at their faces and the way they carried themselves, she recognized that many of the teens had experienced pain and loss in their lives. She wanted to do something, anything, to serve the students.

But unsure of exactly what to do, she decided to pray that someone would rescue the youth in her area. She invited several Christian women to meet and pray for all of the students who attended the high school once a week. The prayer meetings lasted for six years.

Within a few years, an unknown youth minister by the name of Jim Rayburn moved to the area and accepted a position at a local church. The youth meetings he hosted were incredibly popular. Eventually Rayburn felt led to start his own organization in 1941.

Since then, Young Life has grown into an international organization that reaches more than one million teenagers annually through its ministry. To this day, the organization attributes much of its initial success to the faithful prayers of those women.

Through prayer, God can do things we never thought or imagined possible.

It's amazing what grand new days we can usher into our life as well as the lives of others when we choose to pray. Through prayer, God can do things we never thought or imagined possible. Through prayer, we have the opportunity to become part of the greater story of what God is doing in our generation as well as around the world. Through prayer, we have the opportunity to be part of something that will last forever. As we move into all that God has for us, prayer should go with us every step of the way.

1. *What do you like most about prayer? What is the most difficult aspect of prayer for you?*

2. *Have you ever had God answer a prayer in a surprising or unexpected way? Explain.*

3. *What prevents you from spending more time in prayer each day?*

4. *Look up each passage below and record the specific instructions regarding prayer in each one.*

Scripture	Instruction Regarding Prayer
Romans 12:12	_____
	_____
Colossians 4:2	_____
	_____
1 Thessalonians 5:17	_____
	_____

5. Why do you think Scripture encourages us to pray so much? Have you noticed any difference in your life when you pray more often? Explain.

6. Read **Mark 6:30**. What does this verse say the apostles did? In what ways do you use prayer as an opportunity to gather your thoughts and plans for life?

7. The apostle Paul was not shy about asking for prayer. Read
   Romans 15:30–32. How willing are you to ask for prayer
   from other people when you feel it is needed? How willing are
   you to spend time in prayer for others?

8. Read **Ephesians 6:18.** Do you find this command easy or hard
   to fulfill? Explain.

*Prayer is as simple as talking to God and taking time
to listen for His response in our lives. We are invited
to pray at every occasion, every event, every moment.
Prayer helps us to understand God's perspective and
empowers us to fulfill His will.*

Digging Deeper

One of the most popular prayers is the Lord's Prayer, in which Jesus answers the disciple's question of how to pray. Read Matthew 6:9–13. What strikes you about this prayer? Do any particular phrases catch your attention? Explain. Why do you think the prayer Jesus taught His disciples to pray was so simple?

Ponder and Pray

The opening scripture for this lesson comes from Isaiah 30:19: "How gracious he will be when you cry for help! As soon as he hears, he will answer you." Have you ever received a gracious response from God when you cried out to Him in prayer? Explain. How have you found this verse to be true in your own life? Does anything ever prevent you from crying out to God? If so, describe.

Bonus Activity

If you have a prayer list that you pray through regularly, take some time to review it and notice all of the prayers God has answered. If you do not have a prayer list, consider making one in a diary or on a blank page in the back of your Bible. Pray faithfully over this list and take note of the many prayers God answers.

Eight

Coming Alive

He who was seated on the throne said, "I am
making everything new!" Then he said, "Write this
down, for these words are trustworthy and true."

REVELATION 21:5

A large investment bank in New York City had several openings in management positions and the company owner decided to hire from within. He gave three of his best employees new accounts. To one, he gave an account with five million dollars to invest. To a second employee, he gave him a smaller but still significant two-million-dollar account. And to the third employee, he gave a one-million-dollar account. Though it wasn't as big as the other two accounts, it was still a huge opportunity for the employee.

Though the company owner had an idea of when he was going to ask for reports on their investments, he didn't give the three employees an exact deadline. He simply gave them the freedom to do what each thought best with the money. The owner went on a family vacation and decided that when he returned he would ask for summary statements from each of the men.

When he returned to the office, he was delighted to discover that the employee who had been given a five-million-dollar account had doubled his investments in a short time and turned it into ten million. He was amazed at the young man's success and quickly gave him a promotion in the company. Then, he checked in with the employee who had been given two million. To his surprise, this employee had also doubled his account. He, too, would move to one of the management positions. Excited at the results, he stopped by the office of the third employee to see what he had done with the million-dollar account.

> *Embracing a grand new day means tapping into your passions, talents, and the gifts God has given you.*

"Boss, I know that you expect a lot out of us as employees," the man stammered. "And I was scared to lose the money, so I just left it alone. The good news is that it's still a million-dollar account."

"That's not good news!" the boss corrected. "I gave you a job to do and you did nothing. The least you could have done is put the funds in a money market account so they earned interest. But since you did nothing, I'm going to take your account and give it to the other employee who has served me well. You're fired."

This story is based loosely on the parable of the talents, a story that Jesus told to His disciples to encourage them to use the resources that God had given them wisely. The tale is a wonderful reminder that God has given us each unique passions, talents, and gifts. While all of our gifts may differ, we are still invited to put them to use and make a difference in the world around us.

Embracing a grand new day means tapping into your passions, talents, and the gifts God has given you. They can no longer rest on a shelf gathering dust, but they are meant to be used to serve and bless others. What gifts is God calling you to use right now?

1. *In the space below, make a list of at least three gifts that you have discovered that God has given you.*

2. *How are you using those gifts right now in your home, church, and community?*

3. *Do you have any gifts that you've buried? Explain.*

4. Read *Matthew 25:14–30.* Which of the servants in the parable do you relate to most?

5. Can you think of someone you know who was given an amazing gift but buried his or her talent? How were others affected because this person buried a talent?

Sometimes embracing the grand new day God has for us takes time and persistence. But God can do great things with those who are faithful.

6. Read **Luke 18:1–6**. Why did the widow win favor with the judge?

7. How do you think the widow felt when she received the news that she had gotten what she asked for? What do you think the widow's grand new day was filled with?

8. As you reflect on this study so far, how do you feel God inviting you to step out into new areas? What grand new day do you feel God nudging you toward?

The grand new day God has for you will undoubtedly tap into your passions, talents, and the gifts you've been given. You are meant to passionately pursue God and all He has for you.

Digging Deeper

Everyone has been given gifts from God that they're designed to use. Read 1 Peter 4:10. In what ways are you putting this verse into practice right now in your own life? Why do you think it's so important to serve and help others with the unique gifts you've been given? Who has served and helped you with one of their gifts recently? What kind of difference did it make in your life?

Ponder and Pray

The opening scripture for this lesson comes from Revelation 21:5: "He who was seated on the throne said, 'I am making everything new!' Then he said, 'Write this down, for these words are trustworthy and true.'" In what ways have you found this to be true in your own life? Why is it important to constantly look for new opportunities to use your gifts? Are there any opportunities to use your gifts and talents today that simply weren't available five years ago? Explain.

Bonus Activity

Find someone else who has a similar gift, talent, or passion as you. During the next week, look for an opportunity where you can put those gifts and talents to work and invite that other person to join you. Share the story of the experience with others.

Nine

A Contagious Hope

Be strong and take heart,
all you who hope in the Lord.

PSALM 31:24

A story is told of a rich plantation owner in Virginia who had several slaves working for him. Together, the slaves were responsible for taking care of the land and his estate. On a particular day, the wealthy landowner discovered one of his slaves doing something that he considered a waste of time: The slave was reading his Bible. The slave owner scolded the slave for neglecting his work. He reasoned that Sunday provided more than enough time to sit around and study Scripture. To enforce his policy, he had the slave whipped and locked up in a shed.

The slave owner happened to pass by the shed later that day. When he did, he could hear the voice of the whipped slave. Curious, the slave owner approached the shed and leaned his ear closely to the wooden wall. As he did, he heard the slave's prayer, a humble plea for God to forgive the unfair and unjust actions of the slave owner. In his prayer, the slave asked that God not only forgive his master, but that God would touch his master's heart, save him, and make him a good Christian. Standing next to the shed, the plantation owner felt the tremendous weight of his wrongdoing. Soon after, he turned to God and became a Christian.

Though he was physically abused, the slave never gave up hope in God. He continued to believe and pray for his master's redemption and salvation. The result was that the master encountered God and embraced a grand new day in his life. The story is a reminder of the power of hope.

When we hope in God, we are hoping in a God who promises He will never leave us or forsake us.

We are encouraged to keep praying for others, including our enemies and those who treat us poorly. Hope is part of the promise of a grand new day. When we hope in God, we are hoping in a God who promises He will never leave us or forsake us. We are hoping in a God who is faithful until the end. And that is a hope that's worth having today and every day.

1. What are some of your biggest hopes for the upcoming year? Consider financial, spiritual, relational, physical, and other areas of your life.

2. Can you think of a time in your life when you wanted to give up? What got you through that difficult time?

3. Look up **Romans 8:24**. Write the verse in the space below:

4. Do you agree or disagree that "hope that is seen is no hope at all"? Explain. What are some unseen things that you quietly hope for?

5. Read **1 Peter 3:15**. *If someone asked you what is the reason for the hope that you have, what would you say?*

6. *Match the scripture with the passage by drawing a line between each scripture and its passage.*

Bible Passage	Scripture on seeking wisdom of others
Psalm 62:5	Remember your word to your servant, for you have given me hope.
Psalm 71:5	You are my refuge and my shield; I have put my hope in your word.
Psalm 119:49	Find rest, O my soul, in God alone; my hope comes from him.
Psalm 119:114	For you have been my hope, O Sovereign Lord, my confidence since my youth.

7. *Reflecting on the passages in the chart above, where did the psalmist find his hope?*

8. *What is the source of the hope that you have? Why do you think hope is so foundational for moving into your grand new day?*

The grand new day God has for you is often preceded and accompanied by hope. One of the greatest hopes God gives us is for the day we will be with Him in heaven.

Digging Deeper

Many of our hopes require us to wait patiently. Read Titus 2:13. Do you find waiting on God comes easily or is hard to do? In what ways do hoping and waiting go hand in hand? Which comes more easily for you? What are you looking forward to most when it comes to spending eternity with God in heaven?

Ponder and Pray

The opening scripture for this lesson comes from Psalm 21:34: "Be strong and take heart, all you who hope in the Lord." How does having hope strengthen your faith? Do you feel stronger when you have hope? Why or why not? In what ways are you hoping in the Lord right now?

Bonus Activity

Spend some time studying the word "hope" in the Bible. Use a concordance or go online to see how many places the word hope is used in Scripture. As you study these passages, ask God to make His hope come alive in you.

An Outpouring of Newness

A grand new day isn't just a one-day occasion, but something God invites us into this day and every day. He offers us the opportunity to experience Him and His ways every day. And you never know what God is going to do next. This final section explores some of the hallmarks of living out all that God has for you.

Ten

Ongoing Renewal

Therefore we do not lose heart. Though outwardly
we are wasting away, yet inwardly we are being
renewed day by day.

2 Corinthians 4:16

The work of God making all things new in our lives is not just a one-time event but an ongoing celebration! God wants a relationship with us every single day. That means we have the opportunity to call out to Him each and every minute. And when we cry out to God through prayer He does amazing things!

He renews our strength. When we are feeling tired, worn out, and ready to give up, God has a way of infusing our hearts and spirits with the energy we need to keep going. He often places people in our lives to help encourage us and fuel us with the courage we need to make a significant difference.

He renews our resolve. Though at times all of us will experience temptation, God gives us the resolve to say "no" to sin and any self-destructive behavior that would short-circuit the work He is doing in our lives. God gives us the resolve to be true to our word, to choose to serve and love even when it isn't returned, and to shut the door on compromising activities.

He renews our faith. All of us will experience moments of doubt. We will find ourselves questioning and even second-guessing what we believe. In those moments, God has a way of renewing His presence in our lives and building up our faith. He has a way of giving us the faith we need when we need to believe most.

> *He has a way of giving us the faith we need when we need to believe most.*

Experiencing the ongoing renewal that God offers is as simple as turning to Him each day. Matthew 6:33, says, "But seek first his kingdom and his righteousness, and all these things will be given to you as well." When you seek God first, you can't help but experiencing the ongoing renewal of a relationship with Him.

1. Has God been doing anything new in your life this week? Today? Describe in the space below.

2. Do you think there are any things in your past that God cannot make new? Explain.

3. Do you think there are any types of limits at all on what it is possible for God to renew, restore, and make new? Explain.

4. Look up Ephesians 4:22–24. Write the verse in the space below:

5. Do you think that becoming more Christ-like is a one-time event or an ongoing process? Why do you think it's so important to put on the "new self" every day?

6. Look up **Psalm 51:10**. Write the verse in the space below:

7. How often do you think the psalmist prayed this prayer? How often do you ask God to renew your spirit, strength, and courage?

8. In the space below, write a prayer to God asking for His ongoing renewal in your life.

The grand new day God has for us is not just a single day as much as it is a lifestyle of living in relationship with God and receiving all He has for us.

Digging Deeper

God does things very differently than the world does them. Read Romans 12:2. What specific activities or disciplines have you found helpful when it comes to having your mind renewed and transformed by God? In your own spiritual journey, have you had to make any changes in your habit or lifestyle so that you no longer conformed to the patterns of this world? Explain.

Ponder and Pray

The opening scripture for this lesson comes from 2 Corinthians 4:16: "Therefore we do not lose heart. Though outwardly we are wasting away, yet inwardly we are being renewed day by day." Which do you consider stronger: your physical body or your spirit? Have you ever known someone whose body was weak, but whose spirit was outrageously strong? Explain. What are some practical ways you can be renewed day by day?

Bonus Activity

In this lesson, you wrote down the words of Ephesians 4:22–24. Over the course of the next week, commit this passage to memory. Look for an opportunity to share this scripture and its impact on you with someone you know.

Eleven

Your Beautiful Story

"For we cannot help speaking about what we have
seen and heard."

ACTS 4:20

Most people are familiar with the name John Grisham. He's one of the world's most commercially successful novelists. With over one hundred million books in print in several dozen languages, he's noted for regular appearances on the *New York Times* best-seller list. In addition to writing compelling stories, he's also known for living his own compelling adventure.

When John Grisham first began writing, he wasn't well received. In fact, his first novel, *A Time to Kill*, was rejected by twenty-eight publishers and agents. When he finally secured an agent and eventually a publishing house, the print run of his first book was a mere five thousand copies. Of those, Grisham purchased one thousand and began selling them himself to bookstores from the trunk of his own car. Yet he never gave up. He wrote a second novel, *The Firm*, which eventually hit the best-seller list and garnered the attention of the publishing world. Since then, many of his books have been made into movies and he has become a household name in the world of publishing.

All of us have a story to tell. Like John Grisham, we may encounter rejection, obstacles, and unexpected challenges, but eventually those become part of our stories and an inspiration to others. No matter where you are in your journey, you have a story to tell of the exciting new work God is doing in your life. And it is a story that needs to be told, because it will invariably give courage and hope to others.

1. *What are your best ways of communicating? Circle the words that best describe you.*

Verbal	*Telephone/Cell phone*	*Written*
Letters/Cards	*Hand gestures*	*E-mail*
Facial Expressions	*Texting*	

Other _____

2. *Do you feel like the story of what God has done in your life is a beautiful story? Why or why not? Is there anything that prevents you from sharing your story more often?*

3. When God is doing new things in your life, do you find it easy or hard to share that news with others? Explain.

4. Read **Isaiah 63:7**. What does Isaiah specifically say he will tell others about?

5. Can you think of anything God has done in your own life that falls under the description of what Isaiah describes? If so, describe in the space below.

6. Read **Jeremiah 20:9**. In what ways can you relate to Jeremiah's description of talking about God? Have you ever felt God's word in your heart "like a fire"? If so, describe.

7. Do you think it's easier to recognize the beautiful story of what God has done in your own life or in the lives of others? Explain.

8. Are there people in your life right now with whom you need to share the beautiful story of what Christ has done in your life? If so, who are they? What's stopping you from sharing your faith?

As you embrace a grand new day today and every day, you have a beautiful story to tell. You have a compelling story that can be shared with countless people around you.

Digging Deeper

Just as God wanted the Israelites to remember all that He had done for them, God wants us to remember all that He has done for us. Read Deuteronomy 11. Why is it important to reflect on what God has done for you, in you, and through you in the past? How does reflecting on these events help strengthen your faith and give you hope?

Ponder and Pray

The opening scripture for this lesson comes from Acts 4:20: "'For we cannot help speaking about what we have seen and heard.'" What have you been seeing and hearing as you've been studying the Bible lately? Who have you been able to share these discoveries with? Is there someone God is nudging you to reach out to in your church and community to share your spiritual journey with?

Bonus Activity

Over the course of the next week, write a love letter to God thanking Him for the beautiful story that He has been writing in and through your life. Allow the letter to be a gift of worship to God for all He has done.

Twelve

A Grand New Day for Others

Now that you have purified yourself by obeying
the truth so that you have sincere love for your
brothers, love one another deeply, from the heart.

1 PETER 1:22

Recent studies show that people in the United States are far more isolated from each other socially than they were even twenty years ago. In fact, it's estimated that one out of every four Americans say they have no one that they can discuss personal troubles or confide in. That's twice as many people as in 1985.

While it's easy to look at those statistics as a growing problem in our country, we can also look at it as a tremendous opportunity! Why? Because there are countless people around you who are waiting for a grand new day! They're waiting for people to become part of their lives—people who will love them, encourage them, and simply live life with them. You have the opportunity not just to bring a grand new day to others, but to experience one for yourself in the process. When you show kindness, offer encouraging words, and help others, you are making a bigger difference than you realize!

You have the opportunity not just to bring a grand new day to others, but to experience one for yourself in the process.

Whether you invite a college student over for lunch with your family after church, stop by the hospital to see someone who has been in an accident, or visit a shut-in, you're demonstrating the love of Christ. Simple activities like picking up the phone to check in with a friend, taking a homemade pie to the family who just moved into your neighborhood, or sending an encouraging card to someone going through a rough time have a way of breathing life, hope, and love into those around you. You may be tempted to think that those are just little things. But in our modern world, those little things are the big things! So go ahead, practice the acts of kindness and compassion that can usher in a grand new day for those around you.

1. When was the last time someone did something little for you that meant a lot? Describe.

2. *When was the last time you did something small for someone else only to discover that it made a big difference? Describe.*

3. *Make a list of your current friendships. How satisfied are you with these friendships? What could you do to improve and deepen them?*

4. *What activities have you noticed help grow friendships the most? How intentional are you about doing these activities?*

5. Read **John 15:9–17**. Why do you think Jesus was so passionate about loving others? Does loving others help you experience more of God? Why or why not?

6. Read **Galatians 5:14**. In what ways is loving others a reflection of your own relationship with God?

7. Read **Galatians 5:22–24**. In the space below make a list of all of the fruits of the Spirit. Which fruit do you find most abundant in your life? Which fruit do you think is the least "ripe" in your life?

8. Read *Colossians 3:14*. In what ways have you seen love lead to unity among people? Do you think it's possible to have true unity without love? Why or why not?

> *A grand new day is not something you can keep to yourself. It's meant to be shared with others. As you love and serve others right where they are, you begin to usher others into their own grand new day through acts of kindness, generosity, encouragement, and love.*

Digging Deeper

Sometimes as we pray for other people we find ourselves filled with the love that God has for them. Read Ephesians 3:14. Have you ever prayed this prayer over someone you know? Why do you think love is so foundational to who God is? What does this say about His character and who He is?

Ponder and Pray

The opening scripture for this lesson comes from 1 Peter 1:22: "Now that you have purified yourself by obeying the truth so that you have sincere love for your brothers, love one another deeply, from the heart." What does it mean to you to have "sincere love" for others? What does it mean to love one another "deeply"? Do you think there is a cost to deep, sincere love? If so, explain. Who is God calling you to love deeply and sincerely?

Bonus Activity

Review the various sessions of this lesson. Do you see any common themes that God has been specifically speaking to you about? Look for opportunities to share what you've been learning with others in your church and community.

Leader's Guide

Chapter 1: The Wake-Up Call

Focus: *God's mercies are new every morning! He awakens us to the reality of His presence in our lives and invites us to know Him even more.*

1. *Answers will vary. This lighthearted icebreaker question is simply designed to get participants talking and connecting with one another.*

2. *Answers will vary, and this early in the study, you can expect participants to speak in general terms. Some may feel God awakening their hearts to get plugged back in a faith community, pray, study the Bible, or participate in other life-giving spiritual disciplines. Others may sense God leading them to do something like restore a relationship or serve in the community.*

3. *Answers will vary, but often when God wakes us up to a new reality of Him or something He wants us to do, He is very persistent. We may try to roll over and go back to bed, but in His love He pursues us and continues to use people and circumstance as well as Scripture to get our attention and draw our hearts back to Him.*

4. *The paralytic was told that his sins were forgiven, and then he was instructed to take up his mat and go home. He obeyed and was healed. One can only imagine the excitement and thrill of being able to take ones' first steps, to run into your own house, to hug and embrace your family. This was a day the paralytic would never forget.*

5. Answers will vary, but it's fair to suggest both the paralytic's friends and the teachers of the law received a wake-up call. The friends were rewarded for their faithful, persistent service to their friend. They were so determined they cut a hole in the roof, and as a reward they got to see their friend healed! But the teachers of the law were the ones who arguably received the biggest wake-up call. They were challenged in their theological beliefs as well as their understanding of who Jesus was. In addition, verse 12 tells us that everyone was amazed at the miracle—a sign that Jesus truly was the Son of God and the promised Messiah. Through this one miracle, Jesus was able to wake up many people to the reality of God.

6. The Bible describes the other Mary's response to the angel's news as "afraid yet filled with joy." It describes their response to Jesus not so much by emotion as a physical response of clasping to Him and worshiping Him. He tells them to be afraid. Though answers to imagining their own responses will vary, this question is designed to encourage participants to recognize that these were real women encountering an empty grace and the resurrected Jesus.

7. "Therefore go and make disciples of all nations, baptizing them in the name of the Father and of the Son and of the Holy Spirit, and teaching them to obey everything I have commanded you. And surely I am with you always, to the very end of the age" (Matthew 28:19–20).

8. Answers will vary. Sometimes God awakens our hearts to the reality of Himself so that we may know Him and His love even more. But sometimes, like in the story of the resurrection, God awakens us to Himself so that we will respond with a specific

action or commissioning. Some participants may share stories of feeling compelled by God to serve in particular ways, give generously to particular causes, or practice a particular spiritual discipline like prayer or Bible study faithfully.

Chapter 2: Awakened

Focus: *God's wants to give each of us a fresh start, but in order to embrace all that He has for us, we have to respond. Often that response includes making a change—whether it's in our habits, our choices, or our attitudes. Sometimes that means we must stop doing things that go against God's commands or start doing things God asks. But the rewards are worth it all!*

1. *Answers will vary for this icebreaker introductory question.*

2. *Answers will vary, but some participants may have made a change in their work, their family life, or even their health. All kinds of things can cause us to change, including the words of a loving (or even unloving) friend, a strong desire to live differently, a crisis, and other situations may be discussed. As you listen to answers, look for any common denominators among the responses.*

3. *Answers will vary, but this question is designed so that participants will interact and discuss some of the details of the passage.*

4. Jesus told the woman to go and sin no more. Whenever we are given the opportunity for a grand new day, a fresh start from God, then we must choose to stop doing the things that cause us to fall short of God's best. Sinning, choosing to disobey God's laws—which are founded in His love and desire to protect us—must stop if we are to walk into all that God has for us.

5. It's impossible to embrace the fullness of what God has for us if we willingly choose to disobey Him. When we break God's laws and commandments, then we are choosing to do things that hurt ourselves, our relationship with others, and our relationship with God.

6. Answers will vary, but the woman can be described in many terms including: thoughtful, concerned, intrigued, persistent, questioning, thirsty, honest, bold, connected, and talkative among others. Encourage participants to explain their responses.

7. The woman left her water jar to tell everyone what she had experienced. The fact that she left her water jar implies she was in a hurry and eager to tell others. Many of the Samaritans believed because of her testimony. Jesus decided to stay in the area and share the good news with the Samaritans.

8. Answers will vary, but this question is designed to remind participants that they can't keep the story of their faith a secret. It's important to share with others. Sometimes in sharing the grand new day God is giving you, others find themselves experiencing a grand new day too!

Chapter 3: Fresh Perspective

Focus: *God's wants to give each of us a fresh perspective. He wants us to see things as He sees them and love others as He loves them. When we embrace a change in perspective, things deep down inside of us shift and we're better able to reflect God to the world around us.*

1. *Answers will vary, but everyone has had an "aha" moment where they suddenly see the world differently. In those instances, our prejudices are often erased, and we begin seeing people as real people rather than just stereotypes or case studies. In those moments, we often learn to love more deeply.*

2. *Anyone who has ever served or volunteered will be able to share stories of heart-touching encounters with those in need.*

3. *When we change our perspective in response to a hurt or loss, often it results in less compassion for others. When we change our perspective in response to an eye-opening encounter or experience with someone, we often gain more compassion.*

4. *Answers will vary. This is a gutsy question to think about and reflect on but it's important to consider. How much are we allowing God to shape our thoughts and desires? How much are we allowing God to give us His heart for people, situations, and circumstances?*

5. *In Jesus God put His whole heart on display. His heart of flesh chose to love people, heal them and restore them. His heart of*

flesh also revealed how to challenge people to draw closer to God.

6. *Answers will vary, but it's intriguing to consider that they were already talking about Jesus when He joined them. It's also interesting that they didn't even recognize Him.*

7. *They described their hearts burning within them. Answers will vary as to experience, but many can relate to a certain excitement to experiencing Jesus and having Scripture come alive as they read and study.*

8. *Answers will vary but this question is designed to help participants share their faith journeys with each other.*

Chapter 4: The Beauty of Redemption

Focus: *God's redemption is truly beautiful. God can make all things new. No matter what has happened in the past, nothing is beyond His redeeming power.*

1. *Answers will vary.*

2. *Answers will vary.*

3. *David set up Uriah to die by placing him at the front of the battle where he knew he was most likely to be killed.*

4. *Answers will vary. Some may suggest that God told Nathan to use a story since he was a prophet. Others may observe that the story was incredibly effective, because it made David see the issue*

from a familiar perspective before he recognized it in himself. The story was very effective because it made David realize how much he had sinned.

5. *David acknowledges his sin. Nathan quickly lets him know that his sins are forgiven, but there are ramifications of the sin. The son born to David will die. Still David pleaded with God for the son's life. When asked why he pleaded with God and refused any care for himself, he still mentioned the possibility that God might be gracious and allow the child to live.*

6. *Answers will vary, but Jesus warns Peter because he knows Peter is going to be tempted and arguably that he is going to fail, but that his failure is not the end of the story. Jesus' words reveal that He loves Peter, He is for Peter, and He wants him to know that, no matter what, He desires a relationship with him.*

7. *Answers will vary, but Peter denied Jesus for fear of being arrested. He denied Jesus because he was on the run and caught off guard by those who asked.*

8. *Answers will vary and may include: curiosity, excitement, anticipation, and hope. Peter denied Jesus, but he was still willing to get up and pursue a relationship with Him. He ran to the tomb with full hope that he would see something, or rather Someone.*

Chapter 5: The Fuel of Forgiveness

Focus: *Forgiveness goes both ways. Not only do we extend forgiveness to others, but we also receive it as a gift. Forgiveness plays an integral role in letting go of the past and moving forward into all God intends.*

1. *Answers will vary, but we can often forgive little things like someone being late, forgetting about a meeting, or making a promise to bring a covered dish but forgetting it. Often these things are easy to overlook, but the bigger things are much more difficult. We may struggle to forgive betrayal, backstabbing, or someone who hurts us physically. As you discuss this question, look for patterns among participants for certain categories of things that seem more unforgivable.*

2. *Answers will vary, but often forgiving ourselves is the hardest thing of all. We may be able to forgive others, but will replay the same mistake that we made in our own minds time and time again.*

3. *Unforgiveness can trap us in the past and allow things that happened to us or things we did define us. Those incidents can become things we base our identities on. Unknowingly, they can consume significant amounts of time and energy. Forgiveness sets us free to move forward and embrace what God has for us today.*

4. *Answers will vary, but Jesus' response of forgiving seventy-seven times is pretty amazing since in that time and culture His answer was infinite. In essence, He is saying you cannot put*

a limit on forgiveness. You must choose to forgive just as you have been forgiven.

5. *Answers will vary.*

6. *Answers will vary.*

7. *Answers will vary, but these last two questions are designed so that participants recognize that at times we play all three roles—the one who lavishly forgives, the one who refuses to forgive, and the one who experiences unforgiveness from others.*

8. *Answers will vary.*

Chapter 6: Pressing the Gas Pedal

Focus: *Moving forward into all that God has for you can be challenging. We have to make sure that we are asking for and listening to wise counsel and lining up our final destination with God's Word. But once we have, we need to press the gas pedal and go for it!*

1. *Answers will vary, but this question is designed to highlight moments of God's leading and faithfulness in the past.*

2. *Answers will vary, but hopefully participants will be able to share opportunities of service that other members of the group didn't know about.*

3. *One can imagine that the transition for Abraham was difficult. Though he obeyed God, there was a lot of work to be done to*

pack and prepare everything. Undoubtedly, some must have thought he was a little strange for heading out to an unknown place. Though the scripture never says Abraham second-guessed his decision, one can estimate that there were a few moments he doubted or questioned his choice.

4. *Answers will vary.*

5. *Answers will vary, but knowing something is from God often makes it easier to respond and make the move.*

6. *Answers will vary and include fear, anxiety, excitement, relief, and joy among other responses.*

7. *Answers will vary. Use this question to discuss the areas of life that participants are least likely to trust God in. Note any consistencies.*

8. *Answers will vary, but people may find themselves braver in areas of work or home life or parenting or other areas.*

Chapter 7: Praying for God's Best

Focus: *Prayer is as simple as talking to God and taking time to listen for His response in our lives. We are invited to pray at every occasion, every event, every moment. Prayer helps us to understand God's perspective and empowers us to fulfill His will.*

1. *Answers will vary. Prayer is powerful and can allow us to feel the joy and peace of God. When we pray, we admit our*

dependence on God and the reality that we can't do it all on our own which is freeing. Struggles in prayer may include getting really honest with God, waiting for an answer, and taking time to listen among others.

2. *Answers will vary.*

3. *Answers will vary, but busyness often tops the list.*

4. *"Be joyful in hope, patient in affliction, faithful in prayer" (Romans 12:12); "Devote yourselves to prayer, being watchful and thankful" (Colossians 4:2); "Pray continually" (1 Thessalonians 5:17).*

5. *Answers will vary, but often prayer changes our perspective and allows us to reconnect with God. Prayer may allow people to sense God's peace, His guidance, His strength. Prayer can change our attitudes, actions, and reactions.*

6. *The apostles gathered around Jesus and reported to Him all they had done and taught. In the same way, we need to gather our thoughts around Jesus through prayer and connect with Him each and every day.*

7. *Answers will vary. Romans 15:30–32 says, "I urge you, brothers, by our Lord Jesus Christ and by the love of the Spirit, to join me in my struggle by praying to God for me. Pray that I may be rescued from the unbelievers in Judea and that my service in Jerusalem may be acceptable to the saints there, so that by God's will I may come to you with joy and together with you be refreshed." If the apostle Paul needed people praying for*

him and asked for their prayers, how much more should each of us?

8. *Ephesians 6:18, says, "And pray in the Spirit on all occasions with all kinds of prayers and requests. With this in mind, be alert and always keep on praying for all the saints." Some will find this easier to do than others.*

Chapter 8: Coming Alive

Focus: *The grand new day God has for you will undoubtedly tap into your passions, talents, and the gifts you've been given. You are meant to passionately pursue God and all He has for you.*

1. *Answers will vary but may include gifts such as painting, sculpting, organizing, speaking, teaching, organizing, performing, cooking, managing, and many others!*

2. *Answers will vary.*

3. *Answers will vary.*

4. *Answers will vary. At times, all of us have probably been each of the servants mentioned.*

5. *Answers will vary, but we all know someone who didn't use his or her gifts to their full potential. For those who completely buried their talents, it is a loss to everyone in the community.*

6. *The widow won favor with the judge because of her persistence.*

7. *The widow was probably thrilled. She may have told all her friends or even thrown a celebration.*

8. *Answers will vary.*

Chapter 9: A Contagious Hope

Focus: *The grand new day God has for you is often preceded and accompanied by hope. One of the greatest hopes God gives us is for the day we will be with Him in heaven.*

1. *All of us hope for something—it may be a new job, a raise at work, a reconciliation in the family, a new child or grandchild, or a healing from a chronic condition among many other things. It's important to note that we also hope for other people.*

2. *Answers will vary, but it's important to highlight the role hope played in those difficult times. Often hope is found in the kind, encouraging words of a friend or the outpouring of love from a community. Hope often has hands and feet. We often offer more hope for others than we realize.*

3. *"For in this hope we were saved. But hope that is seen is no hope at all. Who hopes for what he already has?" (Romans 8:24).*

4. *Answers will vary. On one hand, hope implies that we are looking forward to something that will happen. On the other hand, we may look to things that God has already done and find great hope and courage in them.*

5. *First Peter 3:15 reminds us to set Christ as Lord apart in our hearts. We are to be prepared to explain the reason for the hope we have. It's important to highlight that this is to be done with gentleness and respect. The answer we give will vary based on our personalities and the way we talk, but the reason for our hope is ultimately found in what Jesus Christ has done for us.*

6. *Answers*

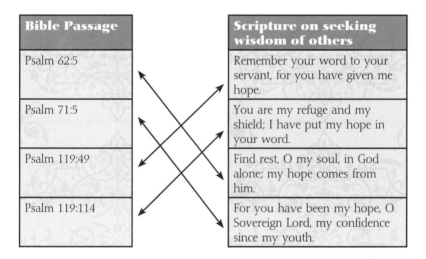

Bible Passage	Scripture on seeking wisdom of others
Psalm 62:5	Remember your word to your servant, for you have given me hope.
Psalm 71:5	You are my refuge and my shield; I have put my hope in your word.
Psalm 119:49	Find rest, O my soul, in God alone; my hope comes from him.
Psalm 119:114	For you have been my hope, O Sovereign Lord, my confidence since my youth.

7. *The psalmist found his hope in God and his words. He is the source of the psalmist's confidence, strength, and hope.*

8. *Answers will vary, but God is the ultimate Source of our hope. But we may look at things that God has done in the past as a source of hope for what God is going to do in the future. Hope gives us the energy and anticipation to move forward into what God has for us.*

Chapter 10: Ongoing Renewal

Focus: *The grand new day God has for us is not just a single day as much as it a lifestyle of living in relationship with God and receiving all He has for us.*

1. *Answers will vary, but this question is designed to help participants recognize that God is always doing something new. He is ever present, ever active, and always doing new things in our hearts, our lives, and our world.*

2. *There are no age limits to God's renewal in our lives. He can work in the life of a seven-year-old, a seventy-year-old, or a seven-hundred-year-old as described in the book of Genesis.*

3. *God can renew and restore anything when we cry out to Him and submit our lives to His will.*

4. *You were taught, with regard to your former way of life, to put off your old self, which is being corrupted by its deceitful desires; to be made new in the attitude of your minds; and to put on the new self, created to be like God in true righteousness and holiness.*

5. *While the moment we make a decision to submit our lives to Christ is a profound and life-changing one, the process of becoming more like Jesus takes a lifetime. That's why it's important to submit our lives and hearts to Him every day, to seek His will and His ways above our own.*

6. *"Create in me a pure heart, O God, and renew a steadfast spirit within me" (Psalm 51:10).*

7. The scripture does not say how often the psalmist prayed this prayer, but undoubtedly, it's a great prayer to pray. When we cry out to God to create a pure heart in us, we are asking Him to bring to the surface the things that are harmful and less than God's best. As those are removed from our lives, we become more like Christ.

8. Answers will vary.

Chapter 11: Your Beautiful Story

Focus: *As you embrace a grand new day today and every day, you have a beautiful story to tell. You have a compelling story that can be shared with countless people around you.*

1. Answers will vary. Encourage participants to use their best ways of communicating in order to share their beautiful story with others.

2. Whether we realize it or not, God is writing a beautiful story in and through us. Even in the hard times, God is doing amazing works of redemption and reconciliation if we allow Him to. Though your story may not seem particularly compelling or beautiful to you, make no mistake—your story is compelling and beautiful to others and to God. We may be embarrassed, shy, or hesitant to share our stories. But when we testify to what God has done in our lives others can't help but be encouraged, challenged, and filled with hope.

3. *Some people may find it easy to share the story of what God is doing just as it's happening, but others may feel more comfortable waiting. Just as some people are happy to show a room in their home that's under construction, others may prefer to wait until the work is complete.*

4. *The kindness of the Lord, the deeds for which He is to be praised, the good things He has done, His compassion, and many kindnesses.*

5. *Answers will vary.*

6. *Answers will vary, but sometimes it's just hard not to talk about God and all the good things He has done. There is something freeing and empowering about talking about God, who He is, and all He has done in our lives. The excitement of talking about God can truly be contagious.*

7. *Often it's easier to recognize the beautiful stories of what God has done in other people's lives rather than our own. But our stories are just as compelling. Though our own journeys may not have as much drama or as many climactic moments as someone else's, make no mistake that others find comfort, joy, and hope in our stories.*

8. *Answers will vary.*

Chapter 12: A Grand New Day for Others

Focus: *A grand new day is not something you can keep to yourself. It's meant to be shared with others. As you love and serve others right where they are, you begin to usher others into their own grand new day through acts of kindness, generosity, encouragement, and love.*

1. *Answers will vary, but this question is designed to highlight the fact that the smallest actions really make a huge impact.*

2. *Answers will vary, but this question is designed to highlight the fact that the smallest actions really make a huge impact.*

3. *Answers will vary.*

4. *Answers will vary but often include everyday activities like taking a walk, going to lunch, canning tomatoes, or simply living life together.*

5. *Jesus makes it clear that just as God loved Him, He loves us. He wants us to remain in that love by obeying His commands. As we do, we will experience His joy, a complete joy. It's interesting to note that Jesus says that the greatest love we can have is when we lay down our lives for each other.*

6. *If you love others as you love yourself then you're in a right relationship with God. But if all your energy is focused on your own life to the exclusivity of others, then God is ready to love*

you in such a way that your love for others becomes a natural extension of the love you've received.

7. *The fruits of the Spirit are love, joy, peace, patience, kindness, goodness, faithfulness, gentleness, and self-control. Answers will vary between the fruit that is the most abundant in their lives and those which are most lacking.*

8. *When we love, it naturally brings people together. Though it's not always in the way that we expect or the timeline that we prefer, love is a powerful force. Apart from love, it's impossible to have the unity God designs for us.*

About the Author

Margaret Feinberg is an author and speaker who offers a refreshing perspective on faith and the Bible. She has written more than a dozen books including *The Organic God* and *God Whispers*. She also wrote The Women of Faith Bible Study *Overcoming Fear*. Margaret is a popular speaker at women's events, luncheons, and retreats as well as national conferences including Catalyst, LeadNow, Fusion, and the National Pastor's Conference.

She lives in Lakewood, Colorado, in the shadow of the Rockies with her 6'8" husband, Leif. When she's not writing and traveling, she loves hiking, shopping, blogging, laughing, and drinking skinny vanilla lattes with her girlfriends. But some of her best days are spent communicating with her readers.

So if you want to put a smile on her face, go ahead and write her!

Margaret@margaretfeinberg.com

www.margaretfeinberg.com

www.margaretfeinberg.blogspot.com

Tag her on Facebook or follow her on twitter

www.twitter.com/mafeinberg

Additional Resources

What Shall We Study Next?

Women of Faith® has numerous study guides out right now
that will draw you closer to God.

Visit www.womenoffaith.com or www.thomasnelson.com
for more information.

Being Yourself
How Do I Take Off This Mask?

*Jesus said to him, "If I will that he remain
till I come, what is that to you? You follow Me."*

JOHN 21:22, NKJV

Who are you? It's one of the simplest but most difficult questions for anyone to answer. Most people spend their lifetime trying to figure out who they really are. Some of their efforts are healthy and rewarding, but others can be dangerous and even destructive. As a follower of Jesus, you don't have to spend years wondering who you really are! You get to go straight to the source—God—to discover not only who you are but who you are created to be.

If you wanted to truly understand a painting, who would you ask? The person who purchased the painting? The person who framed the painting? The museum curator? While all those individuals may have insight, the best possible person to ask would be the artist. In the same way, God invites you to understand yourself in the light of who He has created you to be.

Why is it so important to go to God to discover who you really are? Because He's the only one who really knows. He created you. He knows you like no other. You have gifts and talents and desires tucked inside of you that you may not even know about, but God does!

In this study, you're going to discover who you really are in God's eyes. You're going to learn how simply being yourself sets others free to be themselves. You will have the opportunity to evaluate the unique strengths, gifts, and talents God has given you and how to better use them to serve and love others. And you're going to recognize the rich fruit that grows naturally in your life when you're simply being yourself.

My hope and prayer for you is that through this study you will begin to see yourself as God sees you—beautiful, redeemed, and wonderfully made.

Blessings,

Margaret Feinberg

Resting in Him
I Need to Slow Down, But I Can't!

*The LORD replied, "My Presence will go with you,
and I will give you rest."*

EXODUS 33:14

Rest. Our souls crave it. Our bodies demand it. Our spirits are renewed through it. Yet rest is one of those treasures that we often don't take the time to enjoy in the busyness of life. As the pace of our modern world speeds up, we find ourselves trying to do more in the same amount of time. Left unchecked, we become experts in efficiency—running hard and fast on the treadmill of life. Our souls grow weary. Our bodies grow weak. Our spirits run dry.

When asked what a person truly needs to survive, most people list air, water, and food, while forgetting that rest is also vitally important to our bodies, minds, and spirits. Rest has the power to transform our attitudes, our actions, and even our activities. When well-rested, we are better equipped to face the challenges as well as the occasional curveball daily life often throws at us.

Meanwhile, the God who formed and shaped us offers us rest—*real rest*—in Him. He invites us to step off the treadmill of life and discover the renewal and restoration that can only come from Him. When we take time to rest, we begin to realize that what feels like doing nothing is really allowing God to do something inside of us. Our souls are given a chance to renew. Our physical bodies are given a chance to heal. Our spirits are given the opportunity to connect with God. In those precious moments, we are reminded not just of who we are but whose we are. Afterward, we find ourselves echoing a common response, *I needed that!*

The ultimate rest you will ever experience doesn't just take place during a nap or a lazy Sunday afternoon. Instead, it's found in God. He is the One who renews your weary soul. He is the One who gives you strength when you think you can't go any farther—emotionally, physically, spiritually, and relationally. The rest that God provides is like no other. Don't you think it's time that you take a break and enter into the rest God has for you?

My hope and prayer is that through this study, you will discover real rest—the kind that God has specifically designed for you—and learn to relax in the arms of your Savior.

Blessings,

Margaret Feinberg

WOMEN OF FAITH
DEVOTIONAL JOURNAL

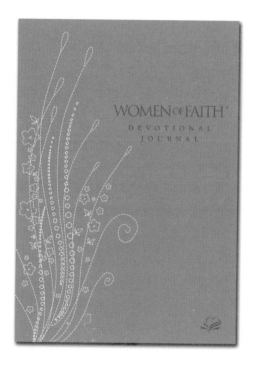

*T*he *Women of Faith Devotional Journal*
speaks directly to the subject of God's infinite grace. Filled with
stirring quotes and uplifting Scripture, this journal is the ideal
addition to any devotional time.

- SCRIPTURE VERSES HIGHLIGHT WISDOM FOR DAILY LIFE

- YOUR FAVORITE WOMEN OF FAITH SPEAKERS' ENLIGHTENING
  THOUGHTS ON GRACE

- PLENTY OF WRITING SPACE TO RECORD DREAMS, HOPES,
  AND PERSONAL REFLECTIONS

WOMEN OF FAITH

THOMAS NELSON
Since 1798